Baby and Beyond

Progression in Play for Babies and Children

About Me

Published 2009 by A&C Black Publishers Limited
36 Soho Square, London W1D 3QY
www.acblack.com

ISBN 978-1-4081-1245-8
Text © Clare Beswick 2009
Series Editor: Sally Featherstone Illustrations © Martha Hardy 2009

A CIP record for this publication is available from the British Library.

Printed in Great Britain by Latimer & Company Limited

This book is produced using paper that is made from wood grown in managed, sustainable forests. It is natural, renewable and recyclable.
The logging and manufacturing processes conform to the environmental regulations of the country of origin.

To see our full range of titles
visit www.acblack.com

Contents

Introduction

This book gives ideas for introducing and extending activities and experiences for babies and young children that help build their social, emotional and personal development. Each page spread contains a range of experiences and a selection of ideas for each of the developmental stages of the Early Years Foundation Stage (EYFS). Developmental stages 4, 5 and 6 have been combined over two sections:

0-11 months

Developmental Stage 1

8-20 months

Developmental Stage 2

16-26 months

Developmental Stage 3

22-40 months

Developmental Stages 4 and 5

40-60+ months

Developmental Stages 5 and 6

Being special, feeling unique, being confident and secure, feeling acknowledged and affirmed by important people are some of the essential needs of all babies and young children and are fundamental to their personal, social and emotional development and well-being.

For all babies and young children this starts with relationships within the family. When a baby or young child meets early years practitioners in a home or group early years setting, positive relationships with key practitioners and other children become critical. There is much practitioners can do to enable children to develop positive relationships and to promote a sense of belonging. As babies and young children are immersed in emotionally supportive environments, self assurance naturally grows. This enables children:

- to meet new experiences and challenges from a secure base
- to cope with distress and stress
- to express emotions and feelings
- to respond to the emotional needs of others
- to view themselves and others positively
- to develop a positive view of themselves and others

Practitioners are central to developing individual babies and children's emotional well-being. You will be conscious of your power as a role model in the way that you behave in your relationships with children, parents and other practitioners.

As well as planning appropriate, carefully planned child-initiated and adult led activities, individual and in small groups, practitioners can ensure that the environment is truly an enabling environment where independence, support and positive relationships are universally the priority.

The activities proposed in this book are carefully planned to match the different developmental stages identified in the EYFS. Practitioners can reflect on the activities and fine tune them to the needs, schemas and learning styles and emotional development of individual children in their key group.

The key person for each baby and child in the EYFS has a particular responsibility to ensure babies and young children feel well cared for, nurtured and safe. Tuning into the needs and personality of each individual member of their key group is critical for the nominated key person. The activities outlined in this book will help practitioners focus on how babies view themselves. This will enable practitioners to build a genuine bond with the child which will form the foundation of a supportive, positive relationship throughout the EYFS.

Young babies (0-11 months)	Babies (8-20 months)	Young children (16-26 months)	Children (22-40 months)	Older children (40-60+ months)

Developmental Stage 1	Developmental Stage 2	Developmental Stage 3	Developmental Stages 4 & 5	Developmental Stages 5 & 6

So Special

Feeling special, unique and valued is vital to all babies and children from birth. Get to know each child as an individual and provide opportunities to show them how treasured and important they are as a person, to others in the group and to the wider community. Help babies and children to recognise their individuality and what makes them who they are.

Young babies (0-11 months)

Greet each baby with their own song. Use the tune of a familiar song or rhyme and adapt the words to make them special to each baby. Try using the tune to 'Hot cross buns' to sing 'Hello name, hello name, tickle on the nose, tickle on the nose, hello name'. Take a few moments to spend some quiet time with the baby observing how they are feeling and thinking about the different ways they are communicating with you.

Developmental Stage 1

Babies (8-20 months)

Create a treasure basket of the baby's own objects, such as a glove, a sock, hat, spoon, cup, soft book, favourite teddy and so on. Spend time exploring these objects together. Talk about possession, such as 'Elsa's hat, peek a boo' and so on. Make time every session for a few moments special one to one time, perhaps dancing together or enjoying a rocking or bouncing on the knee nursery rhyme.

Developmental Stage 2

Young children (16-26 months)

Take a special interest in childrens' homes and families. Make a photo album of simple images with just one item per page, with family, pets, home, special people, favourite toys. Take time to enjoy the album together. Have a special soft toy of your own, and make a few minutes to share this toy with the child, talking about how special and important it is to you. Even a young child will understand this and feel special that you have allowed them such an honour.

Developmental Stage 3

Children (22-40 months)

Make hand and foot prints in paint, with textured paper or with Modroc. Be sure to check for allergies first and supervise carefully to ensure children do not put things in their mouths. Talk about how each print is special and unique to that child. Match each hand or foot print to a photo of the child. Use these to decorate drink and snack time labels, coat pegs or perhaps a treasure box where the child can keep special items they bring to the setting.

Developmental Stages 4 & 5

Older children (40-60+ months)

Draw a simple outline for each child and let them make a montage of images of their favourite toys, animals and books from pictures cut or torn from catalogues and magazines. Listening to each child talk about their favourites and why they make these choices will convey a clear message of interest, respect to the child and help them to feel special and valued. Being an active listener is the key. Make all children feel special by making a birthday chart for the group.

Developmental Stages 5 & 6

Where I Live

Making links with home and family, and experiences outside the home is crucial to a child's learning and development, but also to developing a sense of belonging, a feeling of being part of a wider group or community. Children recognise from a very early age that your interest in their home and culture means that they are valued and important.

Young babies (0-11 months)

Young babies gradually develop an understanding of familiar routines and situations by tuning in to clues from people and their environment. Support these clues by providing simple 'objects of reference', such as giving the baby a spoon to hold a moment or two before mealtimes. Accompany the object of reference (OOR) with a short but consistently used phrase, such as 'dinnertime'. Agree more OORs with colleagues and parents and use then consistently.

Developmental Stage 1

Babies (8-20 months)

Match photos and pictures of familiar objects from homes to actual objects. Introduce lots of simple picture books about homes. Model simple pretend play about putting dolly to bed, or bathing or feeding dolly and so on, including all the familiar routines from the child's own home life. Make sure the objects used are representative of the baby's home life and culture. Give plenty of time for free play with these objects during the day.

Developmental Stage 2

Young children (16-26 months)

Use a simple sung commentary to help young children with emerging simple pretend play. Focus on everyday home based routines, such as getting dressed, bath time, and meals. Use real objects as props and encourage children to imitate your actions. Focus on helping children to use words to describe everyday objects and comment on similarities between what the child has or does at home and the simple pretend play.

Developmental Stage 3

Children (22-40 months)

Use large cardboard boxes to make houses and help the children to make them like their own. Use everyday objects to furnish the homes. Encourage the children to comment on and describe their home and note similarities and differences. Build a miniature town together with key buildings created with Duplo and other construction toys. Focus on familiar people and buildings, such as shops, library, school, park and so on.

Developmental Stages 4 & 5

Older children (40-60+ months)

Extend children's imaginative play with miniatures and play people. Make mini replica houses of their own with shoe boxes and talk with them about similarities and differences between their creations and their homes. Encourage children to draw their front door, add numbers and talk about all the different styles of homes people live in here and around the world. Look at Google images and maps to get a bird's eye view of where the children live.

Developmental Stages 5 & 6

11

My Family

Acknowledging and affirming good relationships within a child's family gives children the confidence to express their feelings and enables children to develop positive ideas about themselves. Such confidence helps children to develop a strong sense of self to cope with new and challenging situations.

Young babies (0-11 months)

Encourage parents to talk about other family members and people who are central in the young baby's world. Greet siblings and include them in saying hello and first play when the baby arrives at nursery. Take time to listen to parents and grandparents and acknowledge the special relationship people have with the baby. Use large clear photos of key people in the baby's life to create a simple album or laminated page for a baby to look at.

Developmental Stage 1

Babies (8-20 months)

Create a treasure basket of special items that belong to key people in the baby's life – mummy's glove, brother's book, grandad's hat etc. Encourage the child to understand and imitate or use simple two word phrases describing possession, such as 'name's shoe' and so on. Consider buying a talking photo album with space for eight photos and a recording facility so each photo has its own personal message for the baby.

Developmental Stage 2

Young children (16-26 months)

Make very simple lift the flap books with photos of family members behind small doors. Share this game with young children, building anticipation as you lift a flap to peek at who is underneath. Play a similar game by hiding photos of key people in the child's life under plastic beakers, so the child can see who is hiding where. Link everyday objects, such as a toy car with an older brother. Look out for small fabric photo albums.

Developmental Stage 3

Children (22-40 months)

Create a simple power point or image gallery slide show of family pictures for children to operate by touching the space bar on a keyboard, or by using a simple switch. Make special card family photo frames for the children to decorate with paint or pictures cut and torn from magazines. Invite family members to come into nursery to show their photographs. Even very young children understand the respect this conveys.

Developmental Stages 4 & 5

Older children (40-60+ months)

Help older children to make simple cubes for dice from a cardboard template. Ask the children to draw a family member or important person in their life's name on a sticker for each face of the dice. Take turns to throw a dice and say something about that person, perhaps something as simple as what colour their hair is, or perhaps what the child likes best about that person, or what they are really good at. Get families to play this game too.

Developmental Stages 5 & 6

Friendships

Even very young babies can enjoy the company of other babies. As children mature and progress through the EYFS, the importance of playing alongside and interacting with peers grows, so that towards the end of the Foundation Stage, children begin to understand the value and importance of supportive, genuine friendship.

Young babies (0-11 months)

Dance with a baby in your arms, facing away from you, while a colleague dances with another baby in a similar fashion. Babies who feel safe and secure will enjoy smiling and reaching for the other baby. Play simple turn taking games with two babies, such as tickling toes, first one baby, then the other, with a simple sung commentary. Give babies plenty of opportunity to be on the floor together for some tummy time. Use double buggies for walks.

Developmental Stage 1

Babies (8-20 months)

Create a big pat mat for babies to share. Roll soft large beach balls in a confined space for babies to reach for and roll or crawl after. Sit two babies together on a large mat with two bags and two sets of objects to explore or post into another box. Observe how the baby's interact and praise good interactions. Encourage babies to stand together looking in a safety mirror, patting their reflections. Play Peek-a-boo together, in a group.

Developmental Stage 2

Young children (16-26 months)

Encourage simple turn taking with posting and tower-building play. Take turns to knock down towers of bricks, or post shapes into a shape sorter. Take turns to pop bubbles, or roll objects down a slope. Start some very simple imitating of simple pretend play, taking turns to give teddy a drink, or wash dolly's hands and so on. Share books with two children and encourage them to hand the books to each other, or to help you hand out items, such as snacks or fruit.

Developmental Stage 3

Children (22-40 months)

Provide lots of opportunities for children to play alongside each other – two children sharing a large sheet of paper, children baking together, two children playing inside a large cardboard box and so on. Provide opportunities where children can play alongside each other, each with their own equipment so there is no anxiety over sharing. Try giving each child a small play bucket of water and a decorator's paintbrush to encourage them to 'repaint' the fence.

Developmental Stages 4 & 5

Older children (40-60+ months)

Share stories and picture books about friends, such as 'All Fall Down' by Helen Oxenbury, or 'Rainbow Fish' by Marcus Pfister. Talk about what makes a good friend and find out what the children like to do with their friends. Circle time offers lots of opportunities to explore what children understand about friendship and to challenge and expand their thinking. Make friendship bracelets and badges together, talking about what being a good friend means.

Developmental Stages 5 & 6

Feeling Good

Prompts, praise and rewards are all important tools to use with babies and children across the whole EYFS to build self confidence and develop a real sense of achievement. Recognising positive behaviour and celebrating effort is critical in enabling young children to become self reliant, motivated and enthusiastic learners.

Young babies (0-11 months)

Engage young babies by offering activities that they can achieve and are developmentally appropriate. Make sure you provide plenty of opportunities and activities that they can do unaided or with minimal help. Praise needs to combine facial expression, eye contact and just one or two key words, combined with a gentle smile and touch. Older babies will enjoy noisy praise, with clapping and much excitement.

Developmental Stage 1

Babies (8-20 months)

At this stage, activities should be short and repetitive with a big reward. Reward babies with an extra turn and make sure that there is much praise for turn taking and pre-verbal skills. Combine words and reinforcing actions, e.g. clap, tickle, pat on the shoulder, hug. Use two or three word phrases consistently to give a very clear message, such as 'great waving' and so on. Develop a sense of achievement and satisfaction with 'You did it!' or 'That's great!'

Developmental Stage 2

Young children (16-26 months)

Rewards at this stage need to be instant and relevant to the activity. Another go is often the best idea – especially when the child has made a great effort and a real achievement. Look at the range of activities provided each session and consider how many can be achieved independently. Plan activities without a fixed outcome where simply having a go is all that is required. A pause, good eye contact and a big smile is a huge individual reward for most.

Developmental Stage 3

Children (22-40 months)

Stickers and stamps are great instant rewards for very young children. They also enable parents and other adults to reinforce the praise and achievement when they see the sticker and give child the opportunity to report back on what they did to achieve the reward. Remember that if the goal is to enable the children to become independent, self-motivated, confident learners, then having a go and using initiative are often more relevant than the accomplishment.

Developmental Stages 4 & 5

Older children (40-60+ months)

Some older children may enjoy collecting stickers and stamps towards a more concrete reward over a period of time, but this depends on the maturity and understanding of the individual child. Non verbal, discreet praise, such as a smile, a wink, thumbs up, or a nod can be as powerful as words. Little jobs and responsibilities are hugely motivating rewards for many children at this stage. Entrusting a child with a special book, toy or message conveys a very powerful message.

Developmental Stages 5 & 6

Exploring Feelings

Tuning in to how babies and young children express their emotions is one of the key roles of the early years practitioner. Enabling babies and children to tune into their own needs and develop ways of expressing their emotions appropriately, and encouraging older children to consider how others may be feeling are significant objectives across the EYFS.

Young babies (0-11 months)

Observe how babies find comfort and are soothed by different objects and people. Note how behaviour, body language and vocalisations are used to express feelings. Ask parents how their baby expresses their feelings to them. Consider how babies reflect the mood around them and can sense the mood of significant adults. Consider how they respond to strong emotions being expressed by other babies in the group.

Developmental Stage 1

Babies (8-20 months)

Babies love looking at photos of other babies. Provide photo books of faces, and comment using very simple short phrases, such as 'Aaahh, baby sad' and so on. Model appropriate language and gesture to accompany the emotions you observe within the group at the setting. Consider body language, gesture and first words babies are using to express their feelings. Take lots of photographs of faces of babies and children in your setting.

Developmental Stage 2

Young children (16-26 months)

Sing simple action songs and encourage simple actions and gestures to introduce words that express feelings. Observe the different ways children at this stage express pleasure, excitement and frustration. How do children let you know they are tired, missing a parent, or hungry? Model appropriate words and gestures to help the children make their feelings understood. Look at resources from Speechmark, e.g. 'Feelings Colour cards'.

Developmental Stage 3

Children (22-40 months)

By now, many children are enjoying simple pretend play and will begin to develop sequences of pretend play around familiar routines, such as bedtime. This is an ideal opportunity to model words to express feelings. Introduce smiley face 'emoticons' on stickers as a way for children to show how they are feeling. Use picture and story books to talk simply about how a character may be feeling. Puppets are a great resource for exploring emotions.

Developmental Stages 4 & 5

Older children (40-60+ months)

Simple circle time games are an excellent vehicle for small groups of children to explore emotions in an enjoyable way. Use Persona dolls to help children understand the feelings of others and to challenge sterotypes. By now, many children are able to begin to understand and comment on other people's emotions. Help them develop an awareness of others through story books and discussion. Look after pets and the environment together.

Developmental Stages 5 & 6

Shared Attention

Sharing delight and becoming absorbed in activities and experiences are important to well-being. Having a good balance of child-initiated and adult directed activity and sustaining attention with other children and adults are vital skills for babies and children to gradually develop across the EYFS.

Young babies (0-11 months)

Capture young babies' visual attention with sharply contrasting black and white visual objects, mobiles and images. Search for black and white baby books, toys and mats. Mirrored toys and reflective objects are ideal to enable young babies to become absorbed and concentrate. Note how individual babies respond to different textures. Consider which they find most fascinating and focus on these. And remember to read to babies from birth.

Developmental Stage 1

Babies (8-20 months)

Treasure basket work is an ideal way to engage the attention of babies at this stage. It enables babies to examine interesting objects using all their senses. Try a treasure basket of reflective objects, and look for toys that encourage the baby to sustain their attention for a few moments. Traditional surprise toys are ideal for this such as 'Jack in the box' and 'Clown on a ladder'. Search reviews of children's books at www.booktrust.org.uk and focus on babies' special interests.

Developmental Stage 2

Young children (16-26 months)

Encourage young children to share their attention with you or one other child at this stage. Such very small group play is ideal to help children sustain their attention while taking turns with another child – pop bubbles, put bricks on a tower, roll balls down a slope. Observe and record the schemas individual children favour and use these when planning follow-up activities for individual children. Read *Again, Again,* by Stella Louis Featherstone.

Developmental Stage 3

Children (22-40 months)

Share visually exciting books with strong rhyming text, or extra features such as lift the flaps or textures to focus and sustain children's attention. Use puppets or suitable props as an additional pull. Finger play also works well at this stage. Play a simple game of gently pressing fingers together, your hand to the child's hand, one by one, and then sing to count to five. Malleable materials from jelly to hardening clay are irresistible to many children at this stage.

Developmental Stages 4 & 5

Older children (40-60+ months)

Involve children in planning activities and follow their lead to give them a sense of ownership of what they are doing. Try parachute and other active games to engage the attention of more active children. Look for suitable PC software that enables children to work together in pairs towards a shared goal. Large art projects are great for enabling children to become absorbed together. Link such projects to themes that the children find most enticing.

Developmental Stages 5 & 6

Making Choices

The opportunity and ability to make choices empowers babies and young children to express their individuality and explore what makes them unique. It enables them to contribute to and challenge their understanding of themselves. Older children will gradually start to recognise the effect their choices has on others.

Young babies (0-11 months)

Observe the ways young babies express their needs and choices – physically, with body language and vocalisations – to different people, environments, circumstances and objects. Model gestures to help them express preferences clearly. Offer real choices, such as holding two small toys in front of them and observing how they let you know their choice – looking, reaching, vocalisations etc. Give them the chosen toy and plenty of praise.

Developmental Stage 1

Babies (8-20 months)

Around 11 months of age, many older babies start to use pointing to indicate choices and also to show you objects of interest. Encourage pointing and gesture, as they are both useful precursors to first words, and will support children in getting their meaning across with unclear words. Consider baby signing as this is a great way to facilitate babies and young children's understanding and expressive language. learn about baby signing at www.singandsign.com.

Developmental Stage 2

Young children (16-26 months)

Use photographs and symbols to represent activities and encourage children to make choices of a preferred activity. Generally at this stage offer choices of two or at the most three objects or photos. Offer choices at snack or mealtimes and encourage parents to offer choices during dressing, such as 'Do you want the blue socks or the red socks?' showing the child the socks and following their choice. This is sometimes easier to do at bedtime than the morning!

Developmental Stage 3

Children (22-40 months)

Choice helps children to feel that they have some control over their lives, and will encourage positive behaviour. Try, 'Do you want to have a drink or your dinner first?', or perhaps, 'Do you want to sit down or stand up while I help you put on your shoes?'. Encourage children to become more independent and individual in their choices. In creative work, offer a range of materials. At story time, choose one book and let the child to choose another.

Developmental Stages 4 & 5

Older children (40-60+ months)

Let children to offer choices to other children, handing out snacks and so on. Tea parties and role play are ideal for this. Ask children to consider the effect of their choice on others, such as 'If you wear the police hat, what can your friend choose?' Visit the local library and browse with children, helping them to consider which are their favourite fact books, story books, poems and so on. Discuss why they have made their individual choices. Tell them which books you like.

Developmental Stages 5 & 6

Relaxing

Being able to feel calm and relaxed is critical to babies and young children's well-being at home and in their early years setting. We all gain physical, psychological and emotional comfort from feeling peaceful and stress free. Look at the different ways you can make this happen even in busy groups.

Young babies (0-11 months)

Baby massage, perhaps just hand or foot massage, is a perfect way to create an atmosphere of calm and tranquillity with individual babies. For small groups of babies, take some advice and experiment with different diffusers of aromatic oils to create a relaxing perfume in the air. Some babies find water play very relaxing at this stage and even playing with wet sponges and warm water can be calming. Create a portfolio of simple rocking rhymes and songs.

Developmental Stage 1

Babies (8-20 months)

Make a recording of traditional lullabies from around the world or buy a book, such as 'Skip Across the Ocean' by Floella Benjamin. Visit your local toy library for some battery operated musical and light cot toys. Babies love to look at gentle slow moving lights as they listen to soft music. Think about your setting and how you can create quiet times and spaces for individual babies. Look at the messages about noise that you all give to the children.

Developmental Stage 2

Young children (16-26 months)

By this stage, many children have found ways to soothe and calm themselves. Make sure there are plenty of quiet corners with big cushions and blankets to snuggle up in. Observe how individual children take themselves off for some quiet time or simply watch what is happening in the group. Some children may seek the comfort of an adult's knee, while others may prefer a rocking toy. Remember the importance of comfort objects to some children.

Developmental Stage 3

Children (22-40 months)

Create a cosy zone. A small corner or den, preferably with a semi transparent covering, where children can watch what's happening in the rest of the setting without being openly observed but still be easily visible to adults. You can use a large cardboard packing carton on its side. Many children like to stroke furry cushions or blankets. Consider what may be most appealing to a tired child needing some rest and relaxation.

Developmental Stages 4 & 5

Older children (40-60+ months)

Use circle time as a time to help children think about what they find calming and relaxing at home and in the group setting. Give each child a cushion or small blanket and all curl up to listen to a story tape together. Often it helps children to relax if they have something to hold. Some children find brushing a doll's hair or soft toy's furry coat very relaxing. Why not all lie down on your backs in the garden on a warm day and simply watch the clouds scudding across the sky?

Developmental Stages 5 & 6

Dressing up and Mirror Play

Dressing up, pretend play and imitating adults in important roles, playing at being mum or dad, grandparents, baby or doctors and nurses are all ways children use to find out about themselves and how they fit into the world around them. Mirror play is a great way to try out lots of faces and is an excellent way of overcoming shyness.

Young babies (0-11 months)

Young babies love to look at their reflection. Play Peek-a-boo and blowing games in safety mirrors. Gather together lots of reflective objects that babies can safely examine. Sing 'Hello *name*' as a baby reaches for and pats his/her own reflection. Give babies hats to put on and tip off their heads and chiffon scarves to peek under. Imitate facial expressions and vocalisations to increase babies' awareness of the sounds and signs they are making.

Developmental Stage 1

Babies (8-20 months)

Stand or sit two babies in front of a large mirror and observe how the babies respond to each other as well as their reflections. Place hats on the babies' heads and play at tipping them off in front of the mirror. Make sure that there is a safety mirror on the wall in your setting that babies can roll or crawl up to and stare at their reflections. Encourage babies to imitate waving 'Bye bye' or raising their arms 'This tall' in front of the mirror.

Developmental Stage 2

Young children (16-26 months)

Create a treasure basket of gloves and mittens for young children to explore. Also try collections of socks, slippers and shoes, or perhaps a collection of accessories such as plastic sunglasses, wigs, bangles and so on. Look out for children with enveloping schemas who love to wrap themselves up in lots of layers, and provide lengths of interesting fabrics. Engage more active children with dressing up outside – make sure clothes release with just a gentle tug.

Developmental Stage 3

Children (22-40 months)

At this stage, children's interest and experiences are mostly focused on home related activities and routines. Provide plenty of opportunities for children to imitate household chores and make sure these are real to the culture and experiences of children in your setting. Provide cut-down but clearly adult clothes for children to try in front of a mirror. Add accessories such as mobile phones, bags, sunglasses, shopping trolleys, satchels, keys, pens, newspapers.

Developmental Stages 4 & 5

Older children (40-60+ months)

By now children are keen to explore the roles of all the people who are important to them, such as postal workers, firemen, police, doctors and nurses, opticians, hairdressers, bus drivers and so on. Provide props, both real and symbolic to facilitate their play. By exploring what it feels like to be in one of these roles, children will be gradually working out what it feels like to be themselves. Visit places of work to get a real understanding of the roles.

Developmental Stages 5 & 6

Active Play

Being confident to try new challenges and knowing your limitations are important goals within the EYFS. Celebrating achievement will encourage children to accept and seek new challenges. Children need to have the confidence to take risks that are outside their comfort zone.

Young babies (0-11 months)

Secure, happy babies will try out new experiences presented gently in a setting in which they feel confident and supported. Introduce new experiences, activities, sights and sounds step by step, at a time of day when the baby is well rested. Observe how the baby tries out and experiments with unfamiliar objects and how they demonstrate a curiosity and desire to explore.

Developmental Stage 1

Babies (8-20 months)

Use music and action rhymes to encourage older babies to try out new movements. Tempt children to move freely around the setting, rolling, crawling, shuffling, walking and so on. Try out new experiences in different positions and on different surfaces, such as crawling on grass or carpet. Offer plenty of tummy time with activities presented at different levels, such as painting sitting on the floor, sitting in a supportive chair, standing at a table or easel and so on.

Developmental Stage 2

Young children (16-26 months)

Try some simple ring games to encourage children to move together as part of a group. Explore crawling through, on and under different surfaces. Try rocking games, such as 'row the boat' and singing games that involve swaying side to side. Remind yourself of all those jigging on the knee rhymes, such as 'Ride a Cock Horse'. Plan a wide variety of messy play and sensory play experiences for children at this age. Each new experience is a small challenge.

Developmental Stage 3

Children (22-40 months)

Encourage children to experiment with different actions. 'Everybody do this just like me' songs and 'Follow my leader' are great activities to encourage imitation. Try some mini 'parachute' type games with small groups of children and a piece of Lycra fabric. The stretchiness makes the game more interesting. Introduce the language of position – in, on, through, between, under – and create mini obstacle courses for children to follow.

Developmental Stages 4 & 5

Older children (40-60+ months)

At this stage children will enjoy co-operative active play, but some find it demanding. Ring games and parachute play are ideal. Ask open questions that encourage children to reflect on what they are doing and how they could work together better. Introduce very simple team games with lots of turn taking. Dream up some whacky races together. Reward all children for their participation and perseverance, as well as success.

Developmental Stages 5 & 6

Music and Dance

Music and dance offers all a unique way to explore and express our feelings. From birth, babies can enjoy music, be soothed and stimulated by it and share the joy of music and dance. Collect music CDs of all sorts and types of music, and sometimes use a radio.

Young babies (0-11 months)

Include music with babies in your planning. Consider the styles of music you play at different times. Use music to soothe and stimulate babies. Play music to accompany a baby gazing at a mobile, and other times match the music to the more active play of older babies. Encourage older babies to experiment with sounds. Hold babies securely and dance together to familiar tunes. And of course, most importantly, sing to babies.

Developmental Stage 1

Babies (8-20 months)

Continue to play a wide repertoire of music to babies. Encourage babies to jiggle about and dance with you. Help them to get absorbed in the music by actively enjoying it together. Sing and hum along and move with the music. Provide lots of interesting sound makers for babies to explore. Use household objects as well as musical instruments. Continue to use relaxing music to soothe babies and accompany quiet moments of rest.

Developmental Stage 2

Young children (16-26 months)

This is a stage of exploring and experimenting. Create treasure basket collections of sound makers. Focus on imitating sounds the child makes and encouraging turn taking. Listen to clocks ticking together and stop to focus on incidental environmental sounds, the plane overhead and so on. Start dancing together, holding hands and sharing the joy of the music. Introduce traditional ring songs and games as well as marching music.

Developmental Stage 3

Children (22-40 months)

Provide musical instruments to experiment with, but also make music with everyday objects from around the setting and outdoors. Think also about the range of sounds children can make with their own bodies, such as stamping feet and so on and incorporate these into action songs and games. Include music makers in the home corner – a pretend radio, a broken mp3 player etc. Put some sheet music in the home corner, with a keyboard.

Developmental Stages 4 & 5

Older children (40-60+ months)

Listen to a range of music from around the world. Talk about what children like about different pieces of music. Get children to talk about music they enjoy at home. Try some Irish dancing, some Scottish jigs and so on. Look at music and dance from other cultures and encourage parents to come and share their traditions. Give children opportunities to hear and try different instruments as well as exploring making music with simple ICT software.

Developmental Stages 5 & 6

31

Circle Time

Babies and young children gradually discover and begin to understand the effect they have others. Over time children build up a picture of themselves defined by the way others respond to them. Focus on building positive interaction between babies and young children to foster good relations.

Young babies (0-11 months)

Plan short bursts of uninterrupted time to devote your total attention to interacting with young babies. Mirror their actions, facial expressions and vocalisations to build a rapport and encourage imitation and turn taking. Show the baby your joy at their responses. Make each baby feel special and cherished by spending time with them, and make sure your key group have plenty of one-to-one time with you.

Developmental Stage 1

Babies (8-20 months)

Begin simple turn taking games, such as taking turns to pop bubbles and so on, with just two older babies. Give babies plenty of opportunities to play alongside each other, each with their own basket of toys. Try big active play and turn taking, perhaps tipping over cardboard boxes, rolling huge inflatable balls and so on. Gradually older babies will discover it is easier to do these things if you do them with a friend.

Developmental Stage 2

Young children (16-26 months)

aTry gentle pulling, tugging, spinning and rolling games with two or three young children, using large pieces of Lycra fabric or hoops. Encourage children to play alongside each other in sand and water play. Try lots of picnic and simple pretend food play, with opportunities for sharing and handing objects to another person. At this stage children love baskets and bags to collect, transport and share out objects, great for social interaction.

Developmental Stage 3

Children (22-40 months)

Play lots of ring games and action rhymes that involve small groups of children, such as 'Five Currant Buns', 'One Elephant Went out to Play' or 'The Farmer's in the Dell'. Use your library or go online for collections and anthologies. Begin games with simple rules, such as 'Follow my leader' where children need to begin to follow a few rules. Imaginative play themes based around 'people who help us' are very important at this stage.

Developmental Stages 4 & 5

Older children (40-60+ months)

Now is the time to build on small group work and try some circle time play. This is the ideal vehicle for children to build confidence and explore issues related to the personal, social and emotional well being. Choose props and activities very carefully. Decide on a short and engaging opening activity linked to the main activity. Establish some rules, such as good listening. Enable children to feel secure in participating or listening, and finish on a positive note.

Developmental Stages 5 & 6

Favourites

Even very young babies are able to express their preferences and begin to explore and establish their individuality. Through the choices made and in the way young children respond to new experiences, we are able to encourage children to believe in themselves and to begin to take control of their destiny.

Young babies (0-11 months)

Watch carefully how babies express their feelings and preferences and note how these are influenced by their environment. Focus on making babies feel safe and secure so they are confident that their needs will be understood. Tuning into young babies' communication is key to this process. Meet regularly with colleagues to ensure that everyone who has regular contact with the baby understands their emerging communication skills and needs.

Developmental Stage 1

Babies (8-20 months)

'All about me' booklets and communication passports are ideal ways to share a baby's preferences and choices with parents, extended family, other practitioners and early years settings that the baby may attend. Find out more about communication passports at www.scope.org.uk. Consider the range of real choices a baby in your setting can make. Ask yourself how you can increase these opportunities and how they can express their choices.

Developmental Stage 2

Young children (16-26 months)

Plan a wide variety of activities for young children at this age, but introduce the new activities gradually so that a young child is not overwhelmed by new resources and too much choice. Show children real objects when asking them to point or vocalise to express a preference. Model and practise offering and making choices as part of personal care routines, such as washing hands – 'The flannel or the sponge?' and so on.

Developmental Stage 3

Children (22-40 months)

Celebrate children's favourites. Record these with pictures and photographs and make displays or books. Create 'My choice' charts, collages and collections. Encourage children to choose and show their favourite book, character in a story, petal on a stem, leaf in the garden and so on. Share your own favourites and say why you have made a particular choice. Praise children for making a choice and being brave enough to think independently.

Developmental Stages 4 & 5

Older children (40-60+ months)

Think about different ways children can express the way they feel about colours, patterns and textures, find favourite songs and musical styles, choose play activities. Consider how their choices are influenced by the schemas they are currently using. Listen and note how their choices are influenced by others and friendship groups. Begin 'Show and tell' sessions, where individual children or friends can show something to the rest of the group.

Developmental Stages 5 & 6

Pretend Play

Babies and young children explore who they are and how they fit in the world through pretend play. First they focus on home and familiar routines, but later role play becomes more imaginative, using symbolic props and exploring the still familiar but wider world of people and places important to the child.

Young babies (0-11 months)

Treasure the young baby's favourite soft toy and enjoy holding baby and toy together and singing simple rhymes together. Encourage older babies to hug their soft toy. Create treasure baskets of simple everyday objects for babies to explore so that they can begin to discover the function of familiar objects, such as a cup for drinking, a shoe to go on a foot and so on. Sing a simple commentary to reinforce the baby's actions as they play with these objects.

Developmental Stage 1

Babies (8-20 months)

Bring together groups of three objects, such as cup, spoon and bowl, or brush, flannel and towel. Play with these with older babies – encouraging the child to imitate simple pretend play and when they are developmentally ready, imitate sequences of simple pretend play, such as brush hair, wash face, dry face and so on. Encourage babies to do these actions to themselves, to you and to dolls or soft toys.

Developmental Stage 2

Young children (16-26 months)

First home corner play enables young children to imitate actions, play alongside older children, and explore familiar everyday objects. They can also experience the satisfaction of being 'in charge' – the one to put the baby to bed, getting to answer the telephone. Keep home corners simple and add new props slowly. Observe how the youngest children watch and imitate the actions of older children and incorporate new actions in their play.

Developmental Stage 3

Children (22-40 months)

Play alongside children in role play situations, drawing comparisons between their home and community based experiences and their play in the early years setting. Help children to create role play scenarios and props that are relevant to their world. Set up a shoe shop, a library, a doctor's surgery. Make sure there are plenty of props so everyone can play an important part. Support children's growing knowledge with relevant fact books.

Developmental Stages 4 & 5

Older children (40-60+ months)

Tuff Spot trays offer a great way to create a huge range of small world play opportunities. Seek inspiration from the children's interests, favourite story books, film and TV. Playing with miniatures enables children to try out imaginary worlds. Plan opportunities for children to play alone and uninterrupted as well as in small groups. Encourage children to select or make their own props. Ask open questions that encourage children to ponder, wonder and reflect.

Developmental Stages 5 & 6

Stories, Poems and Rhymes

Sharing stories, poems and rhymes told from memory or from a book or tape creates a special relationship between the teller and the listener. It is precious time, making babies and young children feel safe, secure and positive. Listening to stories enables them to connect with others' experiences and begin to understand their own place in the world.

Young babies (0-11 months)

Choose books that have something special that will capture the attention of very young babies. Look for board books with textured pages, shiny or reflective bits. Black and white books are very engaging for young babies and encourage their visual attention. Sing finger rhymes and first nursery rhymes gently to babies held facing you and well supported to feel safe and secure.

Developmental Stage 1

Babies (8-20 months)

Use simple props, such as everyday objects and finger puppets to tell short simple stories to babies and to grab attention for action and nursery rhymes. Look for picture and photograph books about babies. Older babies love to look in the faces of other babies! Find books with a surprise on the last page to help babies sustain their attention. Choose action rhymes with big, easily imitated actions and sounds to follow, such as vehicle or animal noises.

Developmental Stage 2

Young children (16-26 months)

Look for stories that focus on homes and everyday experiences. Link images in the picture books with real everyday objects. Support the content of stories with related action rhymes. Enjoy playing with words, encouraging lots of imitation of actions and sounds. Introduce strong rhyming texts and be sure to use a wealth of different voices for your story telling. Help young children to revel in the joy of stories, use props to engage their attention.

Developmental Stage 3

Children (22-40 months)

Now is the perfect time, to introduce children to traditional tales from their own and other cultures so that they can begin to glimpse the huge diversity of the world. Choose books that enable them to explore how characters cope with challenges that are important to them, such as losing a favourite toy, or facing new experiences such as going to the dentist. Make connections between stories, poems and rhymes and their own experiences.

Developmental Stages 4 & 5

Older children (40-60+ months)

Older children can use stories to glimpse other worlds and to face fears and new challenges. Provide a wealth of stories from around the world to introduce children to other cultures and the way other children and families live. Encourage children to explore a wide range of stories and poems, but also to begin to consider what appeals to them about a particular story, developing their own tastes, interests and preferences. The secret is to engage their interest.

Developmental Stages 5 & 6

If you find this book useful you might also like to look at ...

9781408112540

9781408112434

9781905019588

9781906029012

All available from acblack.com/featherstone